Looking at . . . Hypsilophodon
A Dinosaur from the CRETACEOUS Period

THE NEW
DINOSAUR
COLLECTION

For a free color catalog describing Gareth Stevens' list of high-quality books and multimedia programs, call 1-800-542-2595 (USA) or 1-800-461-9120 (Canada). Gareth Stevens Publishing's Fax: (414) 225-0377.
See our catalog, too, on the World Wide Web: http://gsinc.com

Library of Congress Cataloging-in-Publication Data

Coleman, Graham, 1963-
    Looking at— Hypsilophodon / by Graham Coleman; illustrated
by Tony Gibbons. — North American ed.
      p. cm. — (The new dinosaur collection)
    Includes index.
    Summary: Describes the physical characteristics and probable
behavior of this two-legged plant-eating dinosaur built for speed.
    ISBN 0-8368-1732-X (lib. bdg.)
    1. Hypsilophodon—Juvenile literature. [1. Hypsilophodon.
2. Dinosaurs.] I. Gibbons, Tony, ill. II. Title. III. Series.
QE862.O65C646 1997
567.9'7—dc20   96-41851

This North American edition first published in 1997 by
Gareth Stevens Publishing
1555 North RiverCenter Drive, Suite 201
Milwaukee, Wisconsin 53212 USA

This U.S. edition © 1997 by Gareth Stevens, Inc. Created with original © 1996 by
Quartz Editorial Services, 112 Station Road, Edgware HA8 7AQ U.K.

Consultant: Dr. David Norman, director of the Sedgwick Museum of Geology,
University of Cambridge, England.

Additional artwork by Clare Heronneau.

Printed in the United States of America

1 2 3 4 5 6 7 8 9 01 00 99 98 97

Looking at . . . Hypsilophodon
A Dinosaur from the CRETACEOUS Period

by Graham Coleman

Illustrated by Tony Gibbons

THE NEW
Dinosaur
COLLECTION

Gareth Stevens Publishing

MILWAUKEE

Contents

5 Introducing **Hypsilophodon**

6 Small and speedy

8 Elongated skeleton

10 Dinosaur race

12 Look-alikes

14 International dinosaur

16 On the run

18 Getting it right

20 A fast family

22 **Hypsilophodon** data

24 Glossary and Index

Introducing
Hypsilophodon

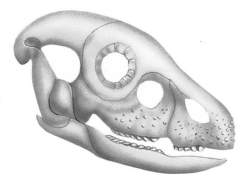

If human beings had existed when the dinosaurs roamed Earth millions of years ago, many of these creatures would no doubt have scared us. They were ferocious carnivores, constantly on the lookout for a meal of meat, for which they would kill.

So where and when did this dinosaur live? How did it spend its day? Who were its enemies? And how do we know what it looked like and how it behaved?

But not all dinosaurs were huge and horrible. Some were more gentle herbivores, surviving only on plants, not flesh. **Hypsilophodon** (HIP-SEE-<u>LOAF</u>-OH-<u>DON</u>) was one of these.

Study the pages that follow, and learn everything scientists have discovered so far about this handsome beast, one of the dinosaur "stars" of author Michael Crichton's book, *The Lost World* — a sequel to *Jurassic Park*.

Hypsilophodon was a small, two-legged, plant-eating dinosaur. From its remains, we know that it lived between 120 and 110 million years ago, in Early Cretaceous times.

Its small head was ideal for an herbivore. It had only small teeth at the front of its beaklike mouth, but its many cheek teeth were useful for chopping up tough leaves and other vegetation. These teeth were even self-sharpening, and new ones grew as they wore out.

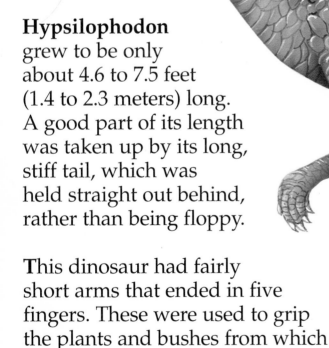

Hypsilophodon grew to be only about 4.6 to 7.5 feet (1.4 to 2.3 meters) long. A good part of its length was taken up by its long, stiff tail, which was held straight out behind, rather than being floppy.

This dinosaur had fairly short arms that ended in five fingers. These were used to grip the plants and bushes from which **Hypsilophodon** fed.

speedy

There were also pouches at the sides of its mouth. Here, **Hypsilophodon** could store some of its food until it was really hungry and ready for a meal. What a convenient picnic basket!

Hypsilophodon had long back legs. This indicates that it could probably run fast. Each foot had four toes that ended in sharp little claws. These must have been useful for gripping the ground.

Elongated

Hypsilophodon's skeleton was typical of the *Ornithischian* (ORN-ITH-ISK-EE-AN) "bird-hipped" dinosaurs. All of them were herbivores.

Hypsilophodon's body was made for speed. Its bones were long and thin, which allowed it to move at a fast pace.

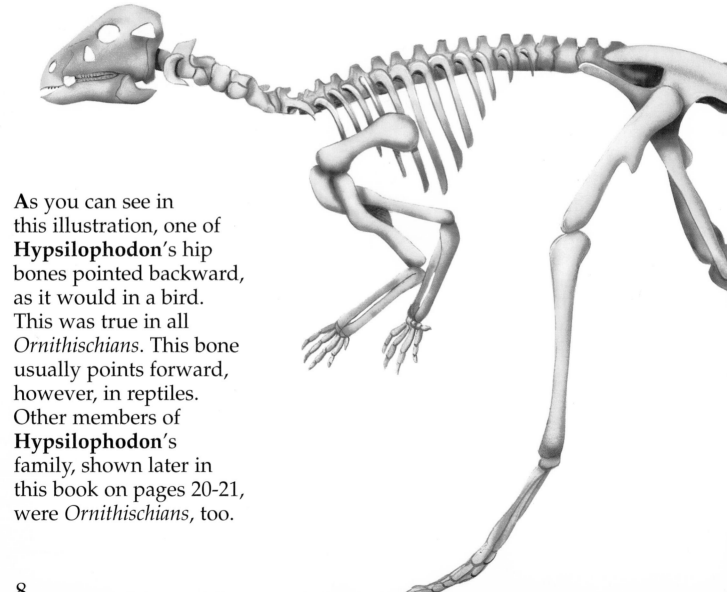

As you can see in this illustration, one of **Hypsilophodon**'s hip bones pointed backward, as it would in a bird. This was true in all *Ornithischians*. This bone usually points forward, however, in reptiles. Other members of **Hypsilophodon**'s family, shown later in this book on pages 20-21, were *Ornithischians*, too.

skeleton

The illustration of its lengthy upper and lower leg bones indicates that **Hypsilophodon** must have taken long strides when running. Its feet also had elongated bones. As well as helping the dinosaur to keep its balance when running, **Hypsilophodon**'s stiff tail could have been used to swipe any threatening predators.

As you can also see from the reconstructed skeleton shown here, **Hypsilophodon**'s skull was small and pointed. It was probably lightweight, which would have meant that **Hypsilophodon** could easily move its head from side to side, as well as up and down — all the better to spot an approaching enemy.

If you look closely at **Hypsilophodon**'s five-fingered hands, you will see that the outer-facing finger was small and stubby, while the other fingers were more suited to scratching and tearing at plants.

Now turn the page to find out how fast **Hypsilophodon** could run.

Dinosaur race

Scientists can get an idea of how fast dinosaurs ran by measuring the distances between the footprints they left behind. The fastest dinosaurs left great gaps between their strides as they sprinted along. By comparing these tracks to those of modern animals running at top speed, experts can estimate how fast each type of dinosaur was able to travel.

So which were the fastest dinosaurs of all? Dinosaurs usually needed to run at high speed for one of two reasons — either to chase their prey or to escape from predators.

Hypsilophodon (**3**) was a speedy little dinosaur, perhaps reaching up to 31 miles (50 kilometers) per hour to avoid an enemy. For this reason, the family to which it belongs is called the "dinosaur gazelles."

Even faster were small, ostrich-like creatures such as **Gallimimus** (GAL-EE-<u>MIME</u>-US) (**2**), which could have sprinted along at 37 miles (60 km) per hour. But perhaps the fastest dinosaur of all may have been **Dromiceiomimus** (<u>DROM</u>-EE-<u>SYE</u>-OH-<u>MIME</u>-US) (**1**), whose name means "emu mimic." Scientists have calculated that it could have run at an amazing 40 miles (65 km) per hour. This speed would surely have won **Dromiceiomimus** a gold medal if there had been dinosaur olympics!

1

2

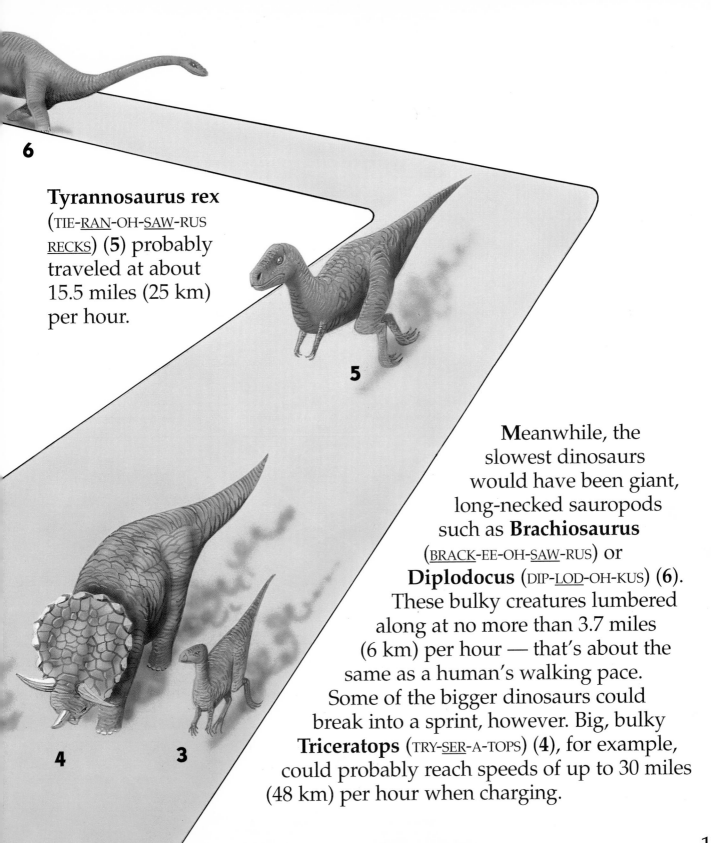

6

Tyrannosaurus rex
(Tie-<u>ran</u>-oh-<u>saw</u>-rus <u>recks</u>) (**5**) probably traveled at about 15.5 miles (25 km) per hour.

5

Meanwhile, the slowest dinosaurs would have been giant, long-necked sauropods such as **Brachiosaurus** (<u>brack</u>-ee-oh-<u>saw</u>-rus) or **Diplodocus** (dip-<u>lod</u>-oh-kus) (**6**). These bulky creatures lumbered along at no more than 3.7 miles (6 km) per hour — that's about the same as a human's walking pace. Some of the bigger dinosaurs could break into a sprint, however. Big, bulky **Triceratops** (try-<u>ser</u>-a-tops) (**4**), for example, could probably reach speeds of up to 30 miles (48 km) per hour when charging.

4   **3**

11

Look-alikes

Hypsilophodon was one of the very first dinosaurs to be discovered. Its bones were dug up on the Isle of Wight, off the southern coast of England, in 1849.

But not until many years later did paleontologists — scientists who study the remains of plants and animals — realize what they had actually found.

Only part of a skeleton had been unearthed, and the bones were handed over first to Gideon Mantell, a famous English scientist, and then to Sir Richard Owen, the man who actually coined the word *dinosaur*.

Both men were confident that the bones belonged to a young **Iguanodon** (IG-<u>WA</u>-NO-DON).

Iguanodon was one of the few dinosaurs already identified at the time. But these adult bones were smaller than an **Iguanodon**'s, so Owen thought they must have come from a baby. But strangely, these smaller-sized bones kept appearing on the Isle of Wight. This led the scientist Sir Thomas Henry Huxley to re-examine earlier beliefs. As a result, he eventually became convinced that he was looking at a completely new dinosaur after all.

Huxley discovered that the new dinosaur was not a baby but a type that was much smaller than **Iguanodon**, as you can see here, and that the shape of its teeth differed, too. In 1869, he renamed the dinosaur **Hypsilophodon foxii**, which means "Fox's high-ridged tooth."

13

International dinosaur

Many dinosaurs have been discovered in only one part of the world. Remains of **Hypsilophodon**, however, have been unearthed in lots of different places, showing that it really moved around.

In all, the bones from more than twenty different **Hypsilophodon** skeletons have been found on the Isle of Wight alone. However, **Hypsilophodon** did not live on a small island all those millions of years ago. Rather, it roamed across a large landmass that has since split up to become not only islands but also the continents we know today, including North America and Europe. This explains why **Hypsilophodon** remains have also been found in Portugal as well as in South Dakota.

It is likely that bones from this creature lay buried in many other places around the world, too. A close relative of **Hypsilophodon** has even been found in the icy wastes of Antarctica.

On the run

The green woodlands of Cretaceous Europe were home to many types of dinosaurs. There was abundant plant life, so the herbivores never went hungry.

Here, the dinosaur **Baryonyx** (BAH-REE-<u>ON</u>-ICKS) liked to catch a meal of fish with its claws.

The carnivorous dinosaurs, meanwhile, hunted for smaller dinosaurs or scavenged. There were also many lakes and rivers, like the one in the picture *above*.

One bright morning, a group of **Hypsilophodon** was browsing on the horsetails and ferns that grew around the lake. Nearby, a lone **Iguanodon** was nibbling on the lower branches of a large conifer.

The **Hypsilophodon** fed quite happily alongside the **Iguanodon**, since it was also an herbivore and would not attack them.

One dinosaur that was not so friendly, however, was meat-eating **Megalosaurus**.

It now sprinted away as fast as its feet would carry it.

Suddenly, one of the group of **Hypsilophodon** spotted this greedy monster as it lurked behind a clump of tall bushes.

Megalosaurus was not a fast runner and had to sneak up stealthily to catch its prey. At once, the keen-eyed **Hypsilophodon** squeaked in alarm, alerting the others.

Alas, they were not all quick enough to escape. The giant **Megalosaurus** lunged toward the nearest **Hypsilophodon** and trapped it by the tail. It wriggled but could not escape. Daily life in the Cretaceous forests was always full of risks like this for smaller dinosaurs.

Getting it right

Ever since dinosaurs were first discovered, scientists have tried to come up with an accurate picture of what these amazing creatures looked like. It has not always been easy, with only incomplete skeletons to work from in many cases. Some odd theories have arisen from time to time as a result. One of the strangest concerned **Hypsilophodon**.

In 1882, a scientist named James Hulke said that it had long fingers and toes and was well-suited to climbing. He therefore declared that **Hypsilophodon** lived in trees.

Other scientists agreed after deciding that **Hypsilophodon**'s first toe pointed in a different direction from its others and so must have been useful for gripping when climbing. They also said that **Hypsilophodon** had arched claws like a modern tree kangaroo, which would have been no good for walking on the ground.

In the 1970s, however, British paleontologist Peter Galton began to put together the bones of **Hypsilophodon** in a new way. He showed that its toes all faced in the same direction after all and that its feet were not those of a tree-dweller.

Scientists now agree that **Hypsilophodon**'s long limbs were those of a fast runner. It also used its stiff tail for balance when it was on the move. Animals that live in trees need flexible tails for gripping; a stiff tail would get in the way.

Today, no dinosaur expert really believes that **Hypsilophodon** — or any other dinosaur — lived in trees. Instead, they lived on the ground, as shown on the facing page, where several of them are trying to escape from the waters of a sudden flood after heavy rain.

A fast family

Although these dinosaurs are posed as if for a portrait, the **Hypsilophodontids** (HIP-SEE-<u>LOAF</u>-OH-<u>DON</u>-TIDS) are a family known for the speed at which they could run. This must have helped them survive over many millions of years, from Late Jurassic to the end of Cretaceous times. The name *Hypsilophodontid* means "high ridge teeth," a reference to the shape of their small, pointed cheek teeth. The best-known member of the family is, of course, **Hypsilophodon (1)**.

Dryosaurus, (<u>DRY</u>-OH-<u>SAW</u>-RUS) **(2)**, another herbivore, was a larger relative of **Hypsilophodon**, growing up to 13 feet (4 m) long. Its remains have been dug up in North America and Tanzania, Africa. Scientists believe that in **Dryosaurus**'s time, these two great continents were linked into one huge landmass. The name **Dryosaurus** means "oak reptile." It lived long before **Hypsilophodon**, in Late Jurassic times, about 140 million years ago.

Zephyrosaurus (<u>ZEF</u>-<u>EYE</u>-ROE-<u>SAW</u>-RUS) (**3**) has a name that means "west wind reptile." It lived in Cretaceous times in the area now known as Montana. It was identified in 1980 from just a skull and a few back bones. Scientists believe this herbivore grew to be about 6 feet (1.8 m) long. It was much smaller than most other members of the **Hypsilophodontid** family.

Tenontosaurus's (TEN-<u>ON</u>-TOH-<u>SAW</u>-RUS) (**4**) name means "sinew reptile." It lived in North America during Early Cretaceous times, about 110 million years ago. **Tenontosaurus** grew to about 21 feet (6.5 m) in length.

Tenontosaurus could probably walk on all fours, but may have run at top speed on its rear legs only.

4

3

Hypsilophodon data

More than twenty **Hypsilophodon** skeletons have been discovered on the Isle of Wight, off the southern coast of England. No one knows for sure why so many have been found in one place. But some scientists have suggested that a herd may have died there together, perhaps trapped in mud or drowned by a sudden high tide. From these skeletons, experts have discovered quite a bit about **Hypsilophodon**'s lifestyle.

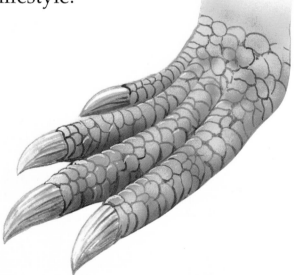

Fast-footed creature

Take a look at the reconstruction of a **Hypsilophodon**'s foot, shown here. From the very long foot bones, we now know that this dinosaur must have been a speedy runner. The claws at the end of its toes would have been used for scratching itself or for gripping the ground. And **Hypsilophodon** ran only on its two back legs.

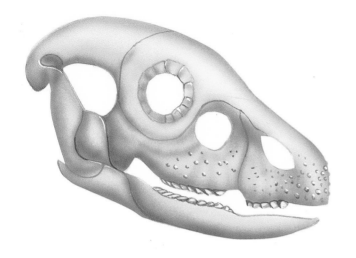

Keen eyesight

Around each eye, **Hypsilophodon** had a ring of small bones. Many reptiles have this, and scientists believe it is a sign of good eyesight. **Hypsilophodon** may therefore have been particularly good at spotting the approach of a carnivorous predator.

Horny beak

With its sharp, horny beak, **Hypsilophodon** could nip off tough leaves and shoots for its vegetarian diet. Behind the beak, **Hypsilophodon**'s numerous cheek teeth were excellent for chewing. What's more, this dinosaur could use its special cheek pouches as a built-in larder, keeping a supply of leaves there until it was hungry again.

Stiff tail

If you look back to pages 8-9, you will see a drawing of a complete **Hypsilophodon** skeleton. Notice how many bony rods were in its tail. These helped to keep the tail stiff so that it could be held off the ground. This must have been very useful for a dinosaur that liked to move at a fast pace! A tail that dragged along the ground would only have slowed it down.

GLOSSARY

carnivores — meat-eating animals.

conifers — woody shrubs or trees that bear their seeds in cones.

herbivores — plant-eating animals.

herd — a group of animals that travel together.

pace — the speed of motion, as in walking or running.

paleontologists — scientists who study the remains of plants and animals that lived millions of years ago.

predators — animals that kill other animals for food.

prey — animals that are killed for food by other animals.

remains — a skeleton, bones, or dead body.

reptiles — cold-blooded animals that have hornlike or scaly skin.

scavenge — to eat the leftovers or carcasses of other animals.

vegetarian — eating only plants or foods made from plants.

INDEX

Baryonyx 16
"bird-hipped" dinosaurs 8
Brachiosaurus 11

carnivores 5, 16, 23
Cretaceous times 6, 16, 17, 20, 21

Diplodocus 11
Dromiceiomimus 10
Dryosaurus 20

Gallimimus 10
Galton, Peter 18

herbivores 5, 6, 8, 16, 17, 20, 21
Hulke, James 18
Huxley, Sir Thomas Henry 13
Hypsilophodon: eating habits of 5, 6, 7, 16, 17, 23; mouth pouches of 7, 23; physical characteristics of 6-7, 8-9; speed of 7, 8, 9, 10, 20, 22; stiff tail of 6, 9, 18, 23; teeth of 6, 23
Hypsilophodon foxii 13
Hypsilophodontids 20, 21

Iguanodon 12, 13, 16, 17
Isle of Wight 12, 13, 14, 22

Jurassic times 20

Mantell, Gideon 12
Megalosaurus 17

Ornithiscians 8
Owen, Sir Richard 12, 13

predators 9, 10, 23
prey 10, 17

sauropods 11
scavengers 16

Tenontosaurus 21
Triceratops 11
Tyrannosaurus rex 11

Zephyrosaurus 21

24